DE   73

W9-BYZ-302

Tree Kangaroo

by Dee Phillips

Consultants:

Lisa Dabek, PhD
Senior Conservation Scientist and Director of the Papua New Guinea Tree Kangaroo Conservation Program
Woodland Park Zoo, Seattle, Washington
www.zoo.org/treekangaroo

Kimberly Brenneman, PhD
National Institute for Early Education Research, Rutgers University, New Brunswick, New Jersey

BEARPORT PUBLISHING

New York, New York

Credits

Cover, © Craig RJD/iStockphoto; 3, © Craig RJD/iStockphoto; 4, © brodtcast/Shutterstock; 5, © Hiroya Minakuchi/Minden Pictures/FLPA; 7, © Imagebroker/FLPA; 8, © Minden Pictures/Superstock; 9, © Craig RJD/iStockphoto; 10, © Jurgen & Christine Sohns/FLPA; 11, © Tim Laman/National Geographic Stock Images; 12T, © Ralph Loesche/Shutterstock; 12B, © Galyna Andrushko/Shutterstock; 13, © Craig RJD/iStockphoto; 14, © Timmy Toucan/Creative Commons; 14–15, © Hans & Judy Beste/Ardea; 16, © Timmy Toucan/Creative Commons and © Craig RJD/iStockphoto; 17, © Craig RJD/iStockphoto; 18–19, © Craig RJD/iStockphoto; 20–21, © Craig RJD/iStockphoto; 23TL, © Sarah Fields Photography/Shutterstock; 23TC, © Hans & Judy Beste/Ardea; 23TR, © Craig RJD/iStockphoto; 23BL, © Timmy Toucan/Creative Commons and © Craig RJD/iStockphoto; 23BC, © Craig RJD/iStockphoto; 23BR, © apiguide/Shutterstock; 24 © Craig RJD/iStockphoto.

Publisher: Kenn Goin
Creative Director: Spencer Brinker
Design: Alix Wood
Editor: Mark J. Sachner
Photo Researcher: Ruby Tuesday Books Ltd

Library of Congress Cataloging-in-Publication Data

Phillips, Dee, 1967–
  Tree kangaroo / by Dee Phillips.
     p. cm. — (Treed, animal life in the trees)
  Summary: "In this book, young readers will learn about the diet, life cycle, behavior and habitat of tree kangaroos. Special emphasis is placed on its habitat"— Provided by publisher.
  Audience: 006-009.
  Includes bibliographical references and index.
  ISBN-13: 978-1-61772-914-0 (library binding)
  ISBN-10: 1-61772-914-0 (library binding)
 1. Tree kangaroos—Juvenile literature. 2. Tree kangaroos—Behavior—Juvenile literature. I. Title.
  QL737.M35P49 2014
  599.2'2—dc23
                                   2013008325

For more information, write to Bearport Publishing Company, Inc., 45 West 21st Street, Suite 3B, New York, New York 10010. Printed in the United States of America.

10 9 8 7 6 5 4 3 2 1

Contents

A Treetop Supper

It is evening in a **rain forest**.

High in the trees, an animal is climbing from branch to branch.

The furry creature is a tree kangaroo.

All afternoon it has been sleeping in a tree.

Now the hungry animal is searching for its supper.

rain forest

tree kangaroo

Tree kangaroos spend a lot of time in trees. They sleep, look for food, and raise their babies high above the ground.

Describe what a tree kangaroo looks like to a friend who has never seen one before.

Where Do Tree Kangaroos Live?

There are 11 different kinds of tree kangaroos.

They all live in rain forests.

One kind is called the Goodfellow's tree kangaroo.

It lives on the island of New Guinea (NOO GIN-ee).

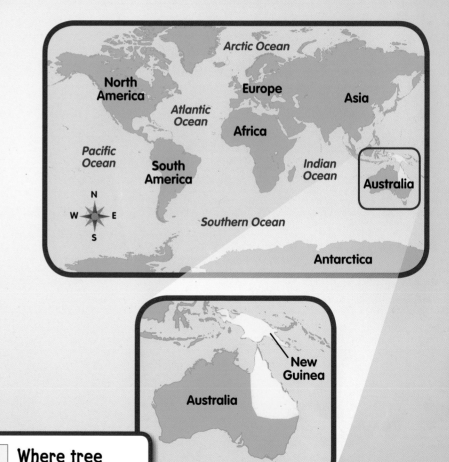

Where tree kangaroos live

Tree kangaroos don't build nests or homes in trees. When it's time to sleep, the animal finds a comfortable place to sit on a branch. Then it simply dozes off.

Goodfellow's tree kangaroo

Meet a Tree Kangaroo

Tree kangaroos have thick, woolly fur.

It can be gray, pale brown, or reddish brown.

The fur of a Goodfellow's tree kangaroo is reddish brown with golden patches.

The furry animal has golden stripes on its back and golden rings on its long tail.

The tail can measure up to three feet (.9 m) long.

stripes

Goodfellow's tree kangaroo

rings

tail

An adult Goodfellow's tree kangaroo measures up to 2.5 feet (76 cm) long from its nose to its bottom. It weighs about 16 pounds (7 kg).

claws

Look at the tree kangaroo's long claws. How do you think having long claws helps the animal?

Life in the Treetops

A tree kangaroo's body is just right for living in trees.

Its strong front legs help it climb up and down tall trees.

Its long, curved claws dig into the **bark** on trees and can grip branches.

As it walks along branches, its long tail helps it stay balanced.

The bottoms of a tree kangaroo's feet are covered in tough, rubbery skin. This special skin helps the animal grip wet branches and stop itself from slipping.

A tree kangaroo finds its food in the treetops. Look at this picture. What foods do you think a tree kangaroo might eat?

Hungry Kangaroos

Tree kangaroos climb and leap from tree to tree, looking for food.

There is lots of food to eat in the rain forest trees.

Tree kangaroos eat leaves, bark, flowers, and fruit.

They also eat moss and ferns, which are plants that grow on trees.

fern

moss

Tree kangaroos mainly look for food in the early morning and in the evening, just before it gets dark.

Giant Leaps

When a tree kangaroo wants to get down from a tree, it makes a huge leap.

Amazingly, it can jump 60 feet (18 m) down to the ground.

That's like jumping off a five-story building!

pouch

Look at the female tree kangaroo in this picture. She has a **pouch**, like a pocket, on the front of her body. What do you think she uses this pouch for?

a tree kangaroo looking for food

Tree kangaroos sometimes climb down or jump out of a tree to look for food on the ground.

In the Pouch

Adult tree kangaroos live alone until it's time to **mate**.

About 44 days after mating, a female gives birth to a tiny baby.

It is called a joey.

The joey climbs into its mother's pouch.

Here, it drinks milk from her body and grows bigger and bigger.

At about five months old, the joey starts to peek out of the pouch.

a male and female tree kangaroo

mother tree kangaroo

A newborn joey is about the size of a jellybean. It has no fur, and its eyes are closed. Its fur grows and its eyes open during the first few months of its life.

a joey in its mother's pouch

17

Raising a Treetop Baby

A mother tree kangaroo licks her joey to keep it clean.

She also licks her pouch to clean it after the joey goes to the bathroom.

As she climbs through trees, the joey inside her pouch stays safe from falling.

At about seven months old, the joey climbs out of the pouch for the first time.

Now it spends some time in the pouch and some time climbing in the trees.

Tree kangaroos belong to a group of animals called **marsupials**. A marsupial gives birth to a tiny baby that is not fully formed. The baby finishes growing inside its mother's pouch instead of inside her body.

mother tree kangaroo

nine-month-old tree kangaroo

19

Growing Up

At about ten months old, a joey no longer rides in its mother's pouch.

Soon it stops drinking her milk, too.

Instead, the joey follows its mother through the trees, eating leaves and other adult foods.

When the tree kangaroo is about 18 months old, it will go off to live alone.

A male will be ready to mate when he is two years old.

When a female is two to three years old, she will be ready to raise her own treetop baby.

Each adult tree kangaroo lives in its own area, called a **home range**. A tree kangaroo has favorite trees in its home range that it uses for resting and sleeping.

15-month-old tree kangaroo

Science Lab

Help the Tree Kangaroos

Tree kangaroos need their treetop homes to survive.

Sadly, rain forest trees are being cut down for wood. The trees are also being cut down to make space to grow crops.

Make a book to tell friends and family members why tree kangaroos need the rain forest.

Think about the questions below. The answers will help give you ideas for facts to put in your book.

- **Where do tree kangaroos sleep?**
- **Where is the main place that tree kangaroos look for food?**
- **What do tree kangaroos eat?**

Make a book about tree kangaroos

1. Have an adult staple two pieces of paper together.

2. At the top of each page, write one reason why tree kangaroos need the rain forest. Draw a picture, too.

3. Share your book with friends and family members.

Tree kangaroos eat foods that grow on trees.

Science Words

bark (BARK) the tough covering on the outside of a tree

home range (HOHM RAYNJ) the area where an animal lives and finds its food

marsupials (mar-SOO-pee-uhlz) a group of animals in which the young are raised in pouches on the mothers' bellies

mate (MAYT) to come together in order to have young

pouch (POUCH) a pocket-like part of a mother tree kangaroo's belly, used for carrying her young

rain forest (RAYN FOR-ist) a place where many trees and other plants grow and lots of rain falls

Index

Read More

Clark, Willow. *Tree Kangaroos (Up a Tree).* New York: Rosen Publishing (2012).

Lawrence, Ellen. *A Kangaroo's Life (Animal Diaries: Life Cycles).* New York: Bearport Publishing (2012).

Miller, Chuck. *Tree Kangaroos (Animals of the Rainforest).* Austin, TX: Steadwell Books (2002).

Learn More Online

To learn more about tree kangaroos, visit **www.bearportpublishing.com/Treed**

About the Author

Dee Phillips lives near the ocean on the southwest coast of England. She develops and writes nonfiction and fiction books for children of all ages. Dee's biggest ambition is to one day walk the entire coastline of Britain—it will take about ten months!